OVERCOMING

SHYNESS

15 *Short and Potent Steps on How to Talk to Anyone, Avoid Awkwardness, and Improve Connection*

Viola Jacob

Copyright © 2023 by Viola Jacob

KINDLY SCAN THIS CODE TO SEE OTHER BOOKS BY THIS AUTHOR AND REACH OUT TO ME FOR ANY ENQUIRIES VIA CONSULTWITHVIOLA@GMAIL.COM

TABLE OF CONTENTS

FROM SHY TO CONFIDENT: A PERSONAL JOURNEY OF EMPOWERING OTHERS

In my journey with my friend Beatrice, I discovered how to help her overcome shyness at work. This experience inspired me to write a guide that's easy to follow, using simple words and no complicated grammar. Beatrice struggled with shyness at her job. Meetings, networking events, and speaking in public made her nervous. She needed someone to help her, and that's when I stepped in. We started by understanding why she felt shy. Beatrice shared her worries and self-doubts, and I listened without judgment.

To tackle shyness, we took it one step at a time. We began with easy conversations and gradually moved to more challenging situations. It was amazing to see Beatrice grow more comfortable with each step. Next, we set small goals that Beatrice could achieve. Celebrating these little victories boosted her confidence. I encouraged her to accept herself and focus on her strengths. We practiced positive thinking to replace her negative thoughts.

As I supported Beatrice, our friendship deepened. Helping her overcome shyness wasn't just about her; it strengthened our bond too. Seeing the positive change in her made me realize that this journey could help others too. That's when I decided to write a simple guide.

The 15 steps in the guide come from Beatrice's experience and what I learned. It's like a roadmap for anyone who wants to feel more confident and beat shyness. This guide isn't full of complicated words or fancy grammar. It's made to be easy to use. Beatrice's story isn't just about overcoming shyness; it's about making connections and discovering the power we all have inside. The guide, ***Overcoming Shyness: 15 Short and Potent Steps on How to Talk To Anyone, Avoid Awkwardness, and Improve Connection***, is for anyone who wants to break free from shyness and find their confidence.

SHYNESS AND ITS IMPACT ON SOCIAL INTERACTIONS

Shyness is a state of unease or nervousness in social settings that is frequently accompanied by a reluctance to interact with people. It can manifest as a fear of judgment, self-consciousness, or a hesitation to speak up or initiate conversations.

The impact of shyness on social interactions is significant. Individuals who struggle with shyness may find it challenging to connect with others, participate in group activities, or express themselves openly. Shyness can lead to missed opportunities for forming friendships, networking, and advancing in both personal and professional spheres.

Overcoming shyness is crucial for personal and professional growth. In personal life, it allows individuals to build meaningful connections, strengthen relationships, and enjoy social experiences without constant anxiety. Professionally, overcoming shyness opens doors to effective communication, collaboration, and leadership opportunities. It can enhance one's ability to network, present ideas confidently, and pursue career advancements. Ultimately, conquering shyness is a key step towards unlocking one's full potential and leading a more fulfilling life.

STEP 1: UNDERSTAND YOUR SHYNESS

Reflect on Your Own Shyness

Understanding your shyness is the first step toward overcoming it. Take a moment to reflect on your experiences and feelings in social situations. Consider the following prompts:

- **Identify Triggers**: Think about specific situations where you feel most shy. Is it during meetings, social gatherings, or when speaking in public? Pinpoint the exact moments that trigger your shyness.

- **Explore Emotions:** Reflect on the emotions associated with your shyness. Do you feel anxious, self-conscious, or fearful? Understanding the emotions tied to your shyness can help you address them more effectively.

- **Patterns of Shyness:** Are there recurring patterns in your shyness? For example, does it intensify in certain settings or with particular people? Identifying patterns can provide insights into the root causes of your shyness.

Recognize Shyness as a Common Trait

It's essential to recognize that shyness is a common human experience, not a unique or permanent limitation. Consider the following perspectives:

- **Normalizing Shyness:** Understand that many people, even those who appear confident, experience moments of shyness. It's a natural part of the human spectrum of social behavior.

- **Temporary Nature:** Recognize that shyness is not a permanent state. It can be addressed and overcome with the right strategies and mindset. Viewing it as a temporary aspect of yourself allows room for growth.

- **Shared Journey:** You are not alone in your journey to understand and overcome shyness. Others have faced similar challenges and successfully navigated through them. Seek inspiration from those who have transformed their shyness into strength.

Self-Reflection

Take out a journal or use a digital document to record your reflections on the prompts above. Answer the following questions:

What specific situations trigger my shyness?

How do I feel emotionally when experiencing shyness?

Are there recurring patterns or themes in my shyness?

How does recognizing shyness as a common trait make me feel?

____

____

Can I recall instances where others have overcome their shyness?
What lessons can I draw from their experiences?

____

____

____

____

____

By reflecting on these questions, you're laying the foundation for a
deeper understanding of your shyness. This self-awareness will be
crucial as you progress through the steps to overcome shyness and
build more confident social interactions.

STEP 2: SET REALISTIC GOALS

Break Down Your Social Goals into Smaller, Achievable Steps

Setting realistic goals is a powerful way to overcome shyness. Instead of aiming for grand achievements right away, focus on breaking down your social goals into smaller, manageable steps. Here's how you can approach it:

- **Identify Specific Social Goals:** Pinpoint the areas where you want to improve. It could be initiating conversations, speaking up in meetings, or attending social events. Be specific about what you want to achieve.

- **Break Goals into Smaller Steps:** Divide each goal into smaller, actionable steps. For example, if your goal is to initiate conversations, the smaller steps could include making eye contact, offering a friendly greeting, and asking open-ended questions.

- **Set a Timeline:** Assign a realistic timeline to each step. Having a timeframe adds structure and accountability to your goal-setting process.

- **Prioritize Goals:** If you have multiple goals, prioritize them based on what feels most achievable or what you believe will have the most significant positive impact on your confidence.

Celebrate Small Victories to Boost Confidence

Celebrating small victories is key to building confidence and reinforcing positive behaviors. Here's how you can turn each achievement into a confidence-boosting moment:

- **Acknowledge Achievements**: Recognize and acknowledge when you successfully complete a step towards your goal. Take a moment to appreciate your effort and progress.

- **Reflect on Growth:** Consider how each small victory contributes to your overall growth. Reflecting on your achievements helps build a positive mindset.

- **Reward Yourself:** Treat yourself to a small reward or engage in a self-care activity when you reach a milestone. This positive reinforcement encourages continued effort.

- **Share Your Success:** If comfortable, share your successes with a friend or supportive individual. Sharing positive experiences amplifies the sense of accomplishment.

Self Reflection Section: Goal Setting and Celebration

Create a goal-setting chart in your book or notepad with the following sections:

Goal: Clearly state your social goal.

____

____

____

____

Smaller Steps: List the smaller, achievable steps you've identified
to reach your goal.

____

____

____

____

Timeline: Assign a realistic timeline for each step.

____

____

____

____

Celebration: Plan how you will celebrate each small victory. It could be a simple acknowledgment, a treat, or a brief moment of self-reflection.

____

____

____

____

____

Reflection: After achieving a goal, reflect on how it felt, what you learned, and how it contributes to your overall growth.

____

____

____

____

____

Regularly update this chart as you progress through your goals. The combination of setting achievable steps and celebrating victories will create a positive momentum, making the journey to overcome shyness more enjoyable and rewarding.

Step 3: Practice Self-Acceptance

Embrace Your Uniqueness

Practicing self-acceptance is a pivotal step in overcoming shyness. It involves embracing your uniqueness and understanding that everyone has their own strengths and weaknesses. Here's how you can foster self-acceptance:

- **Acknowledge Uniqueness**: Reflect on what makes you unique. It could be your talents, interests, or even your quirks. Embrace these aspects as part of what defines you.

- **Avoid Unfair Comparisons**: Resist the urge to compare yourself unfairly to others. Remember that everyone has their own journey and challenges. Focus on your path and celebrate your progress.

- **Learn from Mistakes:** Instead of dwelling on mistakes, view them as opportunities for growth. Accept that making errors is a natural part of the learning process and a chance to improve. Recognize That Everyone Has Strengths and Weaknesses

Understanding that everyone, regardless of outward appearances, has strengths and weaknesses is essential for building a balanced perspective:

- **Avoid Idealizing Others:** Recognize that others may have their struggles, even if they appear confident. Avoid idealizing people and remember that everyone faces challenges.

- **Appreciate Diversity:** Celebrate the diversity of strengths and weaknesses. Just as you have areas where you excel, others have their unique talents. This appreciation fosters a sense of equality and understanding.

- **Build Empathy:** Understanding that everyone has vulnerabilities builds empathy. It creates a more compassionate mindset, both towards yourself and others.

Focus on Your Positive Qualities

Shifting your focus to your positive qualities is a key aspect of practicing self-acceptance. Here's how you can redirect your attention:

- **Make a Positive Qualities List**: Write down your positive qualities, skills, and accomplishments. Focus on what you do well and what others appreciate about you.

- **Challenge Negative Thoughts:** When negative thoughts arise, consciously challenge them with positive affirmations. Remind yourself of your strengths and achievements.

- **Celebrate Small Wins:** Acknowledge and celebrate small successes. Whether it's completing a task or overcoming a social challenge, recognizing your victories boosts self-esteem.

Self Reflection Section: Embracing Uniqueness

Unique Traits: List three unique traits or qualities that define you.

____

____

____

____

____

Challenges and Growth: Reflect on a recent challenge. How did you navigate it, and what did you learn?

____

____

____

____

____

Positive Qualities: Identify three positive qualities or skills you possess.

____

____

____

____

____

Comparisons: Describe a situation where you compared yourself to others. How might you reframe that comparison in a more positive light?

____

____

____

____

____

Celebrating Uniqueness: Plan one way you will celebrate your uniqueness this week. It could be indulging in a hobby or appreciating a personal accomplishment.

____

____

____

____

By engaging in these reflections, you cultivate a mindset of self-acceptance and learn to appreciate the unique qualities that make you who you are. This, in turn, contributes to building the confidence needed to overcome shyness in social interactions.

Step 4: Develop Positive Self-Talk

Challenge Negative Thoughts and Replace with Affirmations

Positive self-talk is a powerful tool in overcoming shyness. It involves challenging negative thoughts and replacing them with affirmations that foster confidence. Here's how you can incorporate positive self-talk into your daily life:

- **Identify Negative Thoughts**: Pay attention to moments when negative thoughts arise, especially those related to shyness. Are you telling yourself you're not good enough or that others will judge you? Identify these thoughts.

- **Question Their Validity:** Challenge the validity of negative thoughts. Ask yourself if there's evidence supporting these thoughts or if they are merely assumptions. Often, negative thoughts are unfounded.

- **Replace with Affirmations:** Develop positive affirmations that counteract negative thoughts. For example, if you think, "I can't speak up in meetings," replace it with, "I have valuable ideas to share, and my voice is important."

Remind Yourself of Past Successes to Build Confidence

Reflecting on past successes is a powerful strategy to build confidence and counteract self-doubt. Here's how you can use your achievements to boost confidence:

- **Compile a Success List:** Create a list of past successes, no matter how small. These could be personal or professional achievements, instances where you stepped out of your comfort zone, or times when you overcame challenges.

- **Regularly Review Your List:** Periodically review your success list to remind yourself of what you've accomplished. Reflect on the skills and strengths you demonstrated during those moments.

- **Draw Confidence from Past Wins:** When faced with a new challenge, draw confidence from your past successes. Remind yourself that you've overcome difficulties before, and you have the capability to do so again.

Self Reflection Section: Positive Self-Talk Practice

Negative Thoughts: Jot down any negative thoughts related to shyness that you've noticed recently.

____

____

____

____

____

Challenge Negative Thoughts: For each negative thought, challenge its validity. Write down evidence that contradicts these thoughts.

____

____

____

____

____

Affirmations: Develop positive affirmations to counteract each negative thought. Make them specific, encouraging, and tailored to your goals.

____

____

____

____

____

Success List: Compile a list of past successes, achievements, or moments where you felt proud. Include both big and small victories.

____

____

____

____

____

Reflection: Reflect on how challenging negative thoughts and using affirmations felt. Did it change your perspective? How might drawing on past successes influence your confidence moving forward?

____

____

____

____

____

By actively engaging in positive self-talk and reflecting on past successes, you're reshaping your mindset to be more optimistic and self-assured. This transformation in thinking is a key step toward overcoming shyness and building the confidence needed for successful social interactions.

Step 5: Gradual Exposure

Start with Low-Pressure Social Situations

Gradual exposure is a systematic approach to overcoming shyness by easing into social interactions. Begin with low-pressure social situations to build confidence and gradually increase the complexity of your challenges. Here's a structured way to implement gradual exposure:

- **Identify Low-Pressure Scenarios:** Choose social situations that feel less intimidating initially. It could be casual conversations with familiar colleagues or brief interactions in a friendly setting.

- **Set Clear Goals:** Define specific, achievable goals for each exposure. For instance, initiating a short conversation or expressing an opinion during a team discussion.

- **Take Small Steps:** Break down your goals into smaller steps. If your aim is to initiate a conversation, start by making eye contact, then progress to offering a friendly greeting, and finally, engaging in a brief chat.

Gradual Exposure Desensitizes Social Anxiety

The process of gradual exposure is designed to desensitize you to social anxiety over time. As you face and overcome manageable challenges, your anxiety diminishes, and you become more comfortable in social settings. Here's how it works:

- **Reduced Anxiety Response:** By exposing yourself gradually to social situations, your brain learns that these scenarios are not as threatening as initially perceived. This reduces the intensity of your anxiety response.

- **Increased Tolerance:** Gradual exposure builds tolerance to social anxiety. Overcoming small challenges boosts your resilience, making it easier to tackle more complex situations.

- **Confidence Building:** Each successful exposure contributes to your confidence. Celebrate these achievements, as they signify progress on your journey to overcoming shyness.

Self Reflection Section: Gradual Exposure Plan

Low-Pressure Scenarios: List three social situations that feel less intimidating to you.

____

____

____

____

____

Specific Goals: Define a clear goal for each exposure scenario. Be specific about what you want to achieve.

____

____

____

____

Breaking Goals into Steps: Break down each goal into smaller, manageable steps. Outline the sequence of actions you'll take in each scenario.

____

____

____

____

Timeline: Set a realistic timeline for each exposure. It could be a weekly or bi-weekly schedule, depending on your comfort level.

____

____

____

____

Reflection: After each exposure, reflect on your experience. What challenges did you face, and how did you overcome them? Note any changes in your anxiety levels.

____

____

____

____

____

By systematically progressing through low-pressure social situations, you'll gradually build the confidence needed to face more challenging interactions. This methodical approach to exposure is a powerful tool in overcoming shyness and social anxiety.

Step 6: Improve Non-Verbal Communication

Work on Maintaining Eye Contact and Open Body Language

Non-verbal communication plays a crucial role in overcoming shyness and fostering positive social interactions. Focus on these key aspects:

- **Maintaining Eye Contact:** Practice making brief but meaningful eye contact during conversations. It conveys confidence and shows that you are actively engaged. Start with short intervals and gradually increase duration.

- **Open Body Language:** Be mindful of your body language. Avoid crossing arms, as it can create a barrier. Instead, keep your body open and relaxed. Aim to face people directly, it signals approachability.

- **Use Appropriate Gestures to Enhance Communication:** Effective use of gestures complements verbal communication and adds depth to your expressions. Integrate natural and subtle gestures to emphasize points or express enthusiasm. Be mindful not to overuse gestures, ensuring they align with the context of the conversation.

Practice Positive Facial Expressions for Approachability

Facial expressions convey a wealth of information about your emotions and intentions. Ensure your expressions are positive and approachable:

- **Smile Genuinely:** Practice smiling genuinely, conveying warmth and friendliness. A sincere smile can create a welcoming atmosphere and ease tension in social interactions.
- **Friendly Eye Expressions:** Experiment with different eye expressions to convey interest and receptiveness. Avoid expressions that may unintentionally communicate discomfort or disinterest.

Self Reflection Section: Non-Verbal Communication Practice

Eye Contact: Record instances where you consciously maintained eye contact during conversations. Note any observations about the impact on the interaction.

____

____

____

____

Open Body Language: Reflect on situations where you intentionally kept open body language. Describe the response from others and your own comfort level.

____

____

____

____

Gestures in Communication: Document situations where you incorporated gestures into your communication. Evaluate how it enhanced the message and the overall interaction.

____

____

____

____

Facial Expressions Practice: Practice positive facial expressions in front of a mirror. Note the expressions that feel most natural and approachable.

____

____

____

Application in Real Conversations: Implement what you've practiced in real conversations. Describe the outcomes, both in terms of your comfort level and the responses from others.

____

____

____

____

____

Regularly revisiting this workbook section will help you refine your non-verbal communication skills and integrate them naturally into your interactions. Improved non-verbal communication enhances your overall social presence and contributes significantly to overcoming shyness.

Step 7: Master the Art of Small Talk

Prepare Open-Ended Questions for Engaging Conversations

Small talk serves as a bridge to deeper connections. Develop the skill of initiating conversations with open-ended questions to keep interactions engaging and meaningful:

- **Open-Ended Questions:** Prepare a list of open-ended questions that encourage detailed responses. These questions prompt more than a simple "yes" or "no" answer, fostering a deeper connection.

- **Tailor Questions to Context:** Consider the setting and context when crafting your questions. Tailor them to the situation to make the conversation more relevant and enjoyable.

Practice Active Listening for Genuine Interest

Active listening is a cornerstone of effective communication. Demonstrate genuine interest in others by practicing these techniques:

- **Maintain Eye Contact:** Keep eye contact to show attentiveness and convey your interest in the conversation.

- **Paraphrase and Clarify:** Repeat or paraphrase what the other person has said to ensure you understand correctly. This not only clarifies information but also demonstrates that you are actively engaged.

- **Ask Follow-Up Questions:** Use follow-up questions to delve deeper into the topic. This shows that you are genuinely interested in the other person's perspective and experiences.

Self Reflection Section: Small Talk Mastery

Open-Ended Question List: Compile a list of open-ended questions you can use in various situations.

____

____

____

____

____

Contextual Tailoring: Practice tailoring questions to specific contexts. For instance, consider questions suitable for a professional setting versus a social gathering.

____

____

____

____

____

Active Listening Practice: Engage in a conversation with a friend or family member. Practice active listening by maintaining eye contact, paraphrasing, and asking follow-up questions. Reflect on the experience afterward.

____

____

____

____

Real-Life Application: Implement your learned skills in a real conversation. Record the open-ended questions you used and pen down your observations about how active listening enhanced the interaction.

____

____

____

____

By consistently practicing the art of small talk and refining your ability to ask open-ended questions, you'll develop a valuable skill set that not only facilitates smoother conversations but also contributes to building meaningful connections.

Step 8: Expand Your Comfort Zone

Challenge Yourself Regularly

Expanding your comfort zone involves intentionally pushing your boundaries and trying new things. Embrace discomfort as a catalyst for growth:

- **Identify Comfort Zone Boundaries:** Reflect on situations or activities that currently fall within your comfort zone. Recognize where you tend to avoid challenges or new experiences.

- **Set Incremental Challenges:** Establish small, manageable challenges that gradually push the boundaries of your comfort zone. Start with activities slightly outside your usual sphere and progressively increase the level of difficulty.

Join Social Groups or Activities Aligned with Your Interests

Engaging in social groups or activities aligned with your interests provides a natural and enjoyable way to connect with others:

- **Identify Interests:** List your hobbies, passions, or areas you'd like to explore. Identify activities or groups related to these interests.

- **Research Local Groups:** Look for local clubs, meetups, or online communities centered around your interests that are near your location. Joining these groups provides a structured and supportive environment for social interaction.

Self Reflection Section: Comfort Zone Expansion Plan

Comfort Zone Boundaries: List three areas or situations currently within your comfort zone.

____

____

____

____

Incremental Challenges: Identify three incremental challenges that push the boundaries of your comfort zone. Specify the steps you'll take to achieve each challenge.

____

____

____

____

Interests Inventory: Compile a list of your hobbies and interests. This can serve as a foundation for identifying potential social groups or activities.

____

____

____

____

Research and Join Groups: Explore local or online groups aligned with your interests. Provide details about the groups you find and your plan to join them.

____

____

____

____

Reflection: After completing a comfort zone challenge or joining a new group, reflect on your experience. Note any changes in your confidence and feelings toward social interactions.

____

____

____

Regularly revisiting and updating this plan will keep you focused on expanding your comfort zone. As you gradually introduce new experiences and connect with like-minded individuals, you'll find your shyness diminishing and your confidence in social situations growing.

Step 9: Learn from Others

Observe Confident Individuals and Adopt Positive Traits

Learning from confident individuals can provide valuable insights into effective communication. Observe and adopt positive traits that resonate with you:

- **Identify Confident Individuals:** Recognize people in your personal or professional life who exude confidence in social situations. Observe their body language, communication style, and how they engage with others.
- **Positive Communication Traits:** Identify specific traits you admire, such as maintaining eye contact, speaking clearly, or expressing ideas with conviction. Integrate these traits into your own communication style.

Seek Advice from Friends or Mentors

Friends and mentors can offer guidance based on their own experiences. Leverage their insights to enhance your social skills:

- **Identify Supportive Individuals:** Reach out to friends, colleagues, or mentors who excel in social situations. Express your interest in improving your social skills and seek their advice.

- **Ask for Personal Experiences:** Inquire about their own journey in overcoming shyness or building confidence. Understand the strategies they employed and the lessons they learned along the way.

Workbook Section: Learning from Others

Positive Traits Observation: List three confident individuals you admire. Identify one positive communication trait from each person that you'd like to incorporate into your own behavior.

____

____

____

____

Integration Strategy: Outline how you plan to integrate these positive traits into your communication style. Consider specific scenarios where you can apply these traits.

____

____

____

____

Supportive Individuals: Identify two friends or mentors you feel comfortable seeking advice from. Reach out to them and express your interest in improving your social skills.

____

____

____

____

Advice and Insights: Record the advice and insights shared by your supportive individuals. Note any actionable steps or strategies they recommend.

____

____

____

____

Reflection: Reflect on how adopting positive traits and seeking advice has influenced your approach to social interactions. Note any positive changes you've observed.

____

____

____

By actively learning from others and incorporating their positive traits, you'll not only enhance your own social skills but also gain valuable perspectives on overcoming shyness. Leveraging the experiences of those who excel in social situations provides practical insights for your own growth.

Step 10: Focus on the Present Moment

In the intricate dance of social interactions, one of the most potent tools in overcoming shyness is the art of mindfulness. Step 10 encourages individuals to embrace the present moment, fostering genuine connections and freeing themselves from the shackles of overthinking past mistakes or worrying about future interactions.

The Power of Mindfulness in Social Interactions

Mindfulness, in essence, is the practice of being fully present and engaged in the current moment. When applied to social situations, it becomes a transformative tool for overcoming shyness. Here's how:

- **Cultivating Presence:** Mindfulness encourages individuals to fully immerse themselves in the present conversation. By actively listening, maintaining eye contact, and tuning into the nuances of the interaction, one becomes more attuned to the needs and cues of others.

- **Reducing Anxiety:** Shyness often stems from anxiety about how one is perceived or fear of potential judgment. Mindfulness helps alleviate this anxiety by redirecting focus to the immediate experience rather than getting lost in self-doubt.

- **Enhancing Emotional Intelligence:** Being present allows individuals to pick up on subtle emotional cues, fostering a deeper understanding of others. This heightened emotional intelligence contributes to more meaningful connections and helps navigate social situations with greater ease.

Avoiding the Traps of Overthinking

One of the common challenges for those grappling with shyness is the tendency to overthink past mistakes or worry excessively about future interactions. Step 10 encourages a shift away from this detrimental pattern of thinking:

- **Letting Go of Past Mistakes:** Mindfulness teaches the art of acceptance. Instead of dwelling on past errors or perceived shortcomings, individuals are guided to acknowledge them, learn from them, and then release them. This mental shift promotes resilience and growth.

- **Quieting Future Worries:** The future can be a breeding ground for anxiety, especially for those navigating social interactions. Mindfulness helps individuals break the cycle of worry by redirecting attention to the current moment. It fosters a sense of control and reduces the overwhelming weight of future uncertainties.

Self Reflection Section: Mindfulness Practice

Incorporate mindfulness into your daily routine with this section:

Mindful Breathing: Practice a brief mindfulness exercise daily. Set aside a few minutes to focus solely on your breath. Pay attention to each inhale and exhale, bringing your awareness back whenever your mind wanders.

Present Moment Awareness: During social interactions, make a conscious effort to stay present. Avoid mentally preparing responses while someone is speaking. Instead, genuinely absorb their words and respond authentically.

Letting Go of Past Mistakes: Reflect on a past social interaction that still lingers in your thoughts. Acknowledge any mistakes made, consider the lessons learned, and consciously choose to let go of any lingering negative emotions.

Future Interaction Visualization: If you find yourself worrying about a future social interaction, visualize it with a positive outcome. Picture yourself confidently navigating the situation, engaging with others, and experiencing success.

Daily Reflection: Maintain a mindfulness journal to record your daily experiences with staying present. Reflect on moments when you successfully embraced the present and note any shifts in your overall mindset.

Embracing the Journey

In the pursuit of overcoming shyness, mindfulness isn't a quick fix but rather a lifelong skill that transforms the way individuals approach social interactions. By focusing on the present moment, individuals can liberate themselves from the constraints of shyness, creating space for authentic connections and personal growth.

Step 11: Embrace Rejection as a Learning Opportunity

In social interactions, rejection is an inevitable thread. Step 11 encourages individuals to reframe their perspective on rejection, recognizing it not as a verdict on their worth but as a profound opportunity for personal growth.

Understanding Rejection as a Part of Life

- **Destigmatizing Rejection:** Rejection is a universal experience, touching every individual at some point in their lives. It's crucial to destigmatize rejection and understand that it doesn't signify inherent inadequacy. Rather, it is a natural aspect of the complex human experience.

- **Separating Rejection from Self-Worth:** Shyness often intensifies the emotional impact of rejection, leading individuals to internalize it as a reflection of their value. Step 11 guides individuals to detach rejection from their self-worth, recognizing that it is more about compatibility, circumstance, or individual preferences.

Learning from Rejections for Personal Growth

Analyzing Patterns and Themes: Rejections, when viewed through the lens of personal growth, become valuable lessons. Analyze patterns and themes that emerge from rejection experiences. Are there recurring situations, behaviors, or aspects that contribute to rejection? This reflective process unveils areas for improvement.

- **Building Resilience:** Embracing rejection fosters resilience. Instead of viewing it as a setback, see it as an opportunity to build strength and perseverance. Resilience is a quality that not only aids in overcoming shyness but serves as a foundational skill in navigating life's challenges.

- **Seeking Constructive Feedback:** In certain situations, seeking constructive feedback after a rejection can provide valuable insights. This proactive approach demonstrates a commitment to growth and a willingness to learn from experiences. Constructive feedback acts as a roadmap for refinement.

Self Reflection Section: Embracing Rejection for Growth

Incorporate reflection and growth into your journey with this workbook section:

Rejection Reflection: Recall a recent rejection experience and document the emotions and thoughts that surfaced. Acknowledge any initial negative feelings and gently redirect focus towards learning.

____

____

____

____

Identify Patterns: Outline rejection patterns by analyzing commonalities in various experiences. Are there specific circumstances, behaviors, or traits that contribute to rejection? Record these observations.

____

____

____

____

Affirmations for Resilience: Develop affirmations that promote resilience in the face of rejection. Craft statements that highlight your ability to bounce back, grow from experiences, and navigate challenges with strength.

____

____

____

____

Constructive Feedback Inquiry: If appropriate, consider seeking constructive feedback after a rejection. Craft questions that invite insights without placing blame. Record any feedback received and reflect on how it aligns with your own observations.

____

____

____

____

____

Personal Growth Action Plan: Outline specific actions you can take to translate rejection into personal growth. This may include setting goals for resilience, addressing identified patterns, or integrating feedback into your self-improvement journey.

____

____

____

____

____

By understanding rejection as an inherent part of life and utilizing it as a stepping stone for personal development, individuals can navigate social interactions with increased resilience, self-awareness, and a deepened understanding of their own strengths and areas for improvement. Embracing rejection as a learning opportunity becomes a catalyst for a more confident and empowered journey.

Notes

Step 12: Volunteer or Join Social Causes

In the pursuit of overcoming shyness, engaging in volunteer work or joining social causes. This step taps into the transformative potential of shared purpose, providing not only a meaningful context for social interactions but also a structured avenue for meeting new people.

Providing a Shared Purpose for Social Interactions

- **Meaningful Connections:** Volunteering or joining social causes inherently aligns individuals with a shared purpose. This shared commitment fosters a sense of camaraderie and connection, creating a supportive environment for social interactions.

- **Common Ground:** Working towards a cause provides an immediate common ground for individuals involved. This shared focus shifts the dynamic of social interactions from potential awkwardness to a collaborative effort towards a greater good.

Making Social Interactions More Meaningful

- **Purposeful Conversations:** Engaging in activities for a cause naturally leads to conversations with depth and purpose. Rather than navigating small talk, individuals involved in social causes often find themselves discussing shared goals, experiences, and the impact of their efforts.

- **Building Lasting Connections:** The shared experience of contributing to a cause creates a foundation for lasting connections. These connections extend beyond the immediate activity, potentially evolving into friendships rooted in a mutual commitment to social change.

Providing a Structured Way to Meet New People

- **Organized Events and Activities:** Volunteer work and social causes often involve organized events and activities. These provide structured settings for meeting new people in a context that goes beyond traditional socializing, making initial interactions more comfortable.

- **Diverse Social Circles:** Social causes attract individuals from various backgrounds and professions, expanding the diversity of social circles. This diversity not only enriches social interactions but also exposes individuals to different perspectives and experiences.

Workbook Section: Volunteer and Connect

Identify Causes of Interest: List social causes or volunteer opportunities that align with your interests. Consider both local and global initiatives that resonate with you.

____

____

____

____

Setting Participation Goals: Define specific goals for your involvement. Whether it's a certain number of volunteer hours per month or attending a set number of social cause events, establish clear objectives.

____

____

____

____

Reflect on Experiences: After participating in volunteer work or social causes, reflect on your experiences. Note the positive aspects, challenges faced, and any personal growth observed.

____

____

____

____

Connect with Like-Minded Individuals: Identify individuals you meet through these activities who share similar values or interests. Reach out to them for casual conversations or to collaborate on future initiatives.

Expand Your Involvement: Outline opportunities to deepen your involvement in causes that resonate with you. This could include taking on leadership roles, suggesting new initiatives, or participating in related events.

By immersing oneself in volunteer work or social causes, individuals not only contribute to positive change but also create an environment where meaningful connections can naturally blossom. This step represents a powerful shift from merely navigating social interactions to actively shaping a fulfilling and purposeful social life.

STEP 13: SEEK PROFESSIONAL HELP IF NEEDED

Recognizing when to seek professional guidance becomes a valuable asset. If shyness significantly impacts one's daily life, seeking the help of a therapist or counselor can be a transformative step toward personal growth, providing personalized strategies and support.

Recognizing the Impact of Shyness on Daily Life

- **Assessing Daily Functioning:** Reflect on how shyness influences various aspects of daily life. Consider its impact on work, relationships, and overall well-being. If shyness becomes a pervasive barrier, hindering personal and professional growth, it may be time to seek professional support.

- **Identifying Persistent Challenges:** If shyness consistently leads to avoidance of social situations, limits career opportunities, or impedes the formation of meaningful relationships, these challenges may require specialized attention. Persistent difficulties in navigating daily life can benefit from professional intervention.

The Value of Professional Guidance

- **Personalized Strategies:** Therapists and counselors specialize in understanding individual challenges. Seeking professional help allows for the creation of personalized strategies tailored to address the root causes of shyness and develop effective coping mechanisms.

- **Safe and Supportive Environment:** Professional settings provide a safe and supportive environment for individuals to explore and express their feelings. This non-judgmental space fosters self-reflection and allows individuals to delve into the underlying factors contributing to their shyness.

- **Skill Development:** Therapists can guide individuals in developing specific social and communication skills. Whether it's assertiveness training, social anxiety reduction techniques, or cognitive-behavioral strategies, professional guidance facilitates skill development essential for overcoming shyness.

Self Reflection Section: Assessing the Need for Professional Help

Daily Impact Assessment: Reflect on specific instances where shyness has impacted your daily life. Identify challenges that persistently hinder your personal or professional growth.

____

____

____

____

Recognize Persistent Patterns: Consider whether there are persistent patterns of avoidance, anxiety, or self-limiting behaviors associated with shyness. Note instances where these patterns have significantly impeded your goals.

____

____

____

____

Emotional Well-being Evaluation: Assess your emotional well-being in relation to shyness. Are there heightened levels of stress, anxiety, or feelings of isolation? Reflect on the emotional toll that persistent shyness may be taking.

____

____

____

____

Consideration of Professional Support: Based on your reflections, consider whether seeking professional help might be beneficial. Evaluate your openness to exploring therapeutic support as a means of addressing and overcoming shyness.

____

____

____

____

____

Create a Professional Support Plan: If you decide that professional support is warranted, outline a plan for seeking help. This may include researching local therapists or counselors, setting up initial consultations, and establishing realistic goals for your therapeutic journey.

____

____

____

____

____

Seeking professional help is not a sign of weakness but a courageous step towards personal growth and well-being. Therapists and counselors offer valuable insights, tools, and support to navigate the complexities of shyness. By addressing the root causes and developing effective strategies, individuals can embark on a transformative journey towards greater confidence and enhanced social interactions.

Step 14: Celebrate Progress

Amidst the journey of overcoming shyness, celebrating progress is very important. Regularly acknowledging and appreciating the strides made in social growth not only provides a morale boost but also reinforces positive behaviors. This step encourages individuals to reward themselves for achieving social milestones, fostering a sense of accomplishment and motivation for continued progress.

The Importance of Acknowledging Progress

- **Building Confidence:** Celebrating progress is a fundamental building block for confidence. It reinforces the idea that positive change is possible and that efforts invested in overcoming shyness yield tangible results.

- **Positive Reinforcement:** Acknowledging progress serves as a form of positive reinforcement. When individuals recognize and celebrate their achievements, it reinforces the behaviors and strategies that contributed to that success, making them more likely to be repeated.

Strategies for Celebrating Progress

- **Setting Milestones:** Break down the journey of overcoming shyness into manageable milestones. These could be small social achievements, such as initiating a conversation or participating in a group activity. Celebrate each milestone reached.

- **Create a Progress Journal:** Maintain a progress journal to document your journey. Record moments of successful social interaction, instances where you stepped out of your comfort zone, and reflections on the positive impact of these actions. Periodically revisit and celebrate your growth.

Rewarding Yourself for Achieving Social Milestones

- **Choose Meaningful Rewards:** Select rewards that hold personal significance. Whether it's treating yourself to a favorite meal, indulging in a leisure activity, or spending quality time with loved ones, choose rewards that resonate with your preferences.

- **Establish a Reward System:** Create a structured reward system for achieving social milestones. Assign specific rewards to different levels of accomplishment. This establishes a clear connection between progress and the positive reinforcement of celebration.

Self Reflection Section: Celebrating Progress

Identify Social Milestones: List social milestones you've achieved during your journey to overcome shyness. These could include specific interactions, events attended, or personal achievements.

____

____

____

____

Reflection on Impact: Reflect on the impact of each milestone. Consider how these achievements have influenced your confidence, social comfort, and overall well-being.

____

____

____

____

Create a Reward Plan: Develop a reward system with a variety of options. Assign specific rewards to different levels of achievement. Ensure that each reward aligns with your interests and preferences.

____

____

____

____

____

Celebration Rituals: Establish rituals for celebrating progress. Whether it's a personal acknowledgment, a moment of reflection, or a physical celebration, define the rituals that will accompany each milestone.

____

____

____

____

____

Incorporate Progress Celebration into Routine: Outline how you will incorporate progress celebration into your routine. Consider setting aside dedicated moments to reflect on achievements and implement chosen rewards.

____

____

____

The journey to overcome shyness is not only about the destination but also about appreciating the steps taken along the way. By actively celebrating progress, individuals cultivate a positive mindset, reinforcing the belief that change is possible and that every effort contributes to personal growth. This celebration becomes a continuous cycle of motivation, propelling individuals forward on their path to social confidence and flourishing interactions.

Notes

Step 15: Cultivate a Positive Social Circle

As the final step in the journey to overcome shyness, Step 15 emphasizes the importance of intentionally shaping one's social environment. Cultivating a positive social circle involves surrounding oneself with supportive and uplifting individuals. This deliberate approach not only offers a foundation of support but also builds a feeling of understanding that is crucial in the continuous quest for social confidence.

The Impact of a Positive Social Circle

- **Emotional Support:** A positive social circle serves as an emotional support system. Surrounding yourself with individuals who uplift and encourage can counteract the effects of shyness and provide a secure space for personal growth.

- **Encouragement for Growth:** Supportive friends and acquaintances are more likely to encourage personal growth and applaud achievements. They contribute to a positive feedback loop, reinforcing efforts to overcome shyness with affirmation and motivation.

Strategies for Cultivating a Positive Social Circle

- **Evaluate Existing Connections:** Reflect on current social connections and assess whether they contribute positively to your well-being. Identify relationships that are supportive, understanding, and align with your goals.

- **Seek Shared Interests:** Cultivate connections with individuals who share common interests or values. Shared hobbies or passions provide a natural foundation for positive interactions and mutual encouragement.

The Role of Boundaries in a Positive Social Circle

- **Establish Healthy Boundaries:** Maintain healthy boundaries within your social circle. Clearly communicate your needs and expectations, and be mindful of how interactions impact your well-being. Establishing boundaries ensures that the relationships you nurture are beneficial and respectful.

- **Let Go of Negative Influences:** Recognize when a relationship becomes detrimental to your journey. If certain individuals consistently undermine your efforts to overcome shyness or contribute to negative self-perception, consider letting go of these influences to make room for positivity.

Self Reflection Section: Building Your Positive Social Circle

Reflection on Current Connections: Reflect on your existing social connections. Identify relationships that contribute positively to your well-being and those that may need adjustment.

Defining Social Goals: Establish clear goals for the kind of social circle you wish to cultivate. Consider the qualities and characteristics you value in supportive relationships.

Identifying Shared Interests: List your interests and passions. Identify potential social circles or groups where you can connect with individuals who share these interests.

Setting Boundaries: Define healthy boundaries for your social interactions. Consider what behaviors or dynamics you find supportive and respectful. Communicate these boundaries openly and assertively.

Let Go of Negativity: Assess if there are relationships in your life that contribute negatively to your journey. Reflect on the possibility of letting go of these influences to create space for positive connections.

A continued commitment to maintaining and fostering a positive social circle is very important. As individuals intentionally surround themselves with support, understanding, and encouragement, they forge a network that becomes a pillar of strength in their ongoing journey to overcome shyness. Cultivating a positive social circle is not just a concluding step; it is a perpetuating force for continuous growth and flourishing social interactions.

Notes

Conclusion: Embracing the Journey to Social Confidence

As we conclude this guide on overcoming shyness, it's essential to reflect on the transformative journey we've embarked upon together. Each step has been a deliberate stride toward cultivating social confidence, breaking free from the constraints of shyness, and fostering meaningful connection with others. Let's recap the key steps that compose this roadmap to personal growth:

We began by acknowledging shyness as a common trait, dispelling the notion that it is an insurmountable barrier. Recognizing shyness as a temporary state, rather than a permanent limitation, set the foundation for the transformative journey ahead. Breaking down social goals into achievable steps and celebrating small victories marked the second step. This approach allowed for incremental progress, reinforcing the belief that overcoming shyness is an attainable, step-by-step process.

Self-acceptance and positive self-talk encourage embracing uniqueness, focusing on positive qualities, and challenging negative thoughts. By fostering self-acceptance and practicing positive self-talk, individuals began reshaping their internal dialogue, laying the groundwork for improved self-esteem. Step 5 introduced the concept of gradual exposure, helping desensitize individuals to social anxiety. Concurrently, the importance of non-verbal communication was highlighted, emphasizing the impact of body language, gestures, and facial expressions on social interactions.

Mastering small talk guides individuals in mastering the art of small talk, fostering engaging conversations through open-ended questions and active listening. Simultaneously, expanding comfort zones encouraged the expansion of comfort zones, challenging individuals to step outside familiar boundaries and explore new social territories. Learning from Others and Focusing on the Present Moment urged individuals to observe confident individuals, adopting positive communication traits and emphasized the power of mindfulness, encouraging individuals to stay present and engaged in social interactions, freeing themselves from the burden of past mistakes and future worries.

Recognizing when professional help is needed became the focus of Step 13, emphasizing that seeking guidance is a courageous step toward personal growth. Step 14 encouraged individuals to celebrate progress, acknowledging and rewarding the milestones achieved on their journey.

Cultivating a Positive Social Circle highlighted the significance of intentionally shaping a positive social circle. By surrounding oneself with supportive and uplifting individuals, the journey to overcome shyness is reinforced with encouragement and understanding.

As we close this guide, I invite you to reflect on the incredible strides you've made. The journey to overcome shyness is not a linear path; it's a continuous cycle of growth, learning, and self-discovery. Embrace the process of personal development, and remember that setbacks are stepping stones to success. In the pursuit of social confidence, you've equipped yourself with valuable tools, strategies, and a resilient mindset.

Embrace each day as an opportunity for progress, surround yourself with positivity, and celebrate the unique journey that is yours alone. Social confidence is not an endpoint but a dynamic, ongoing evolution. Embrace the journey, and may each step bring you closer to the vibrant, socially confident life you envision.

Notes